The ABCs of Taxes: A Guide for Absolute Beginners

By Jan Charles

1

Contents

Chapter 1: Taxes 101 -– Understanding the Basics

Taxes can be confusing and overwhelming, but they are a necessary part of our society. In this chapter, we'll break down the basics of taxes and help you understand what you need to know.

What Are Taxes?

Taxes are an essential part of any modern society. They are the means by which the government is able to can fund the many public services and programs that we all rely on. These services range from basic necessities such as road maintenance and public schools to more complex services like healthcare, defense, and social security.

When we pay taxes, we are essentially contributing to a communal pool of funds that are then allocated towards various programs and services that benefit society as a whole. This means that taxes are a way for us to invest in our collective future, ensuring that our communities and country continue to thrive and grow.

Without taxes, it would be impossible for the government to provide the wide range of services and programs that we have come to expect. Our roads would be left in disrepair, our schools would lack resources, and the most vulnerable members of society would be left without basic healthcare and social safety nets.

It's important to note that the government uses our tax dollars in a responsible and efficient manner. They are accountable for how they allocate funds and must ensure that they are being used for the benefit of ~~society as a whole~~society. In addition, taxes are often structured in a way that those who earn more income pay a higher percentage of their income in taxes, which helps to create a more equitable society.

While no one likes paying taxes, it's important to understand that they play a vital role in ensuring the stability and well-being of our communities and our ~~nation as a whole~~nation. By paying our fair share, we are investing in a brighter future for ourselves and for generations to come.

In the United States, there are three main tax collecting agencies.

Internal Revenue Service (IRS): The IRS is a federal agency that is responsible for collecting taxes on behalf of the federal government. The agency is responsible for enforcing tax laws and regulations, processing tax returns, issuing tax refunds, and collecting delinquent taxes. The IRS is primarily funded by the federal government, and it has regional offices and local offices throughout the country to help taxpayers with their tax-related questions and concerns.

State Tax Agencies: Each state has its own tax agency that is responsible for collecting state taxes. State tax agencies are responsible for enforcing state tax laws, processing state tax returns, and collecting delinquent taxes. State taxes may include income taxes, sales taxes, property taxes, and other state-specific taxes. State tax agencies are typically funded by state governments, and they may have regional offices or local offices to help taxpayers with their state tax-related questions and concerns.

Local Tax Agencies: In addition to federal and state taxes, local governments may also collect taxes and fees to fund local services and programs. These taxes may include property taxes, sales taxes, business license fees, and other local fees and taxes. Local tax agencies are typically funded by local governments, and they may have offices or departments that handle tax-related questions and concerns. The structure and responsibilities of local tax agencies can vary depending on the jurisdiction, with some cities or counties having dedicated tax departments and others incorporating tax collection into other departments, such as finance or revenue.

Who Pays Taxes?

When it comes to taxes, earning income is one of the most common triggers for tax liability. This includes a wide range of income types, including wages from a job, self-employment income, rental income, and income from investments like stocks or bonds. Even if you're not working, you may still be subject to taxes on certain items like sales tax on purchases or property taxes on a home.

The amount of tax you owe is typically based on the amount of income you earn. The more you earn, the higher your tax rate will be. However, the tax system is often structured so that those who earn less income pay a smaller percentage of their income in taxes, while those who earn more income pay a higher percentage. This is designed to create a more equitable society and ensure that everyone pays their fair share.

It's important to note that there are many different types of taxes, each with their own unique rules and regulations. Federal income tax is one of the most well-known and important types of taxes, but there are also state and local taxes, payroll taxes, and capital gains taxes, among others.

WHAT IS A W-4?

A W-4 is a form that employees use to inform their employers how much federal income tax to withhold from their paychecks. The form includes information about the employee's personal and financial situation, such as their marital status, number of dependents, and other income. Based on this information, the employer calculates how much tax to withhold from the employee's paycheck and remits it to the government on their behalf.

The purpose of the W-4 form is to ensure that employees have enough federal income tax withheld throughout the year so that they do not owe a large amount of taxes when they file their tax return. By adjusting the withholding amount on the W-4 form, employees can ensure that they are paying the correct amount of tax based on their specific circumstances.

Each type of tax is designed to serve a specific purpose, and understanding the nuances of each can help you make better financial decisions.

One important aspect of taxes to keep in mind is that the tax code is constantly changing. This means that it's important to stay up to date on new tax laws and regulations that may affect you. This can be challenging, as the tax code is often complex and difficult to understand, but there are many resources available to help you navigate the system.

Ultimately, taxes are a necessary part of modern society, and understanding your tax obligations is an important part of financial literacy. By taking the time to learn about taxes and how they work, you can ensure that you're meeting your tax obligations while also making informed decisions about your financial future.

WHEN TO DO A NEW W-2

It's important for employees to update their W-4 form whenever their personal or financial situation changes, such as when they get married or have a child. This helps ensure that the correct amount of tax is withheld and can prevent the need for a large tax bill at the end of the year.

Overall, the W-4 form is an important tool for both employees and employers to ensure that the correct amount of federal income tax is withheld from each paycheck.

How Your Taxes Work

Filling out a W-4 form: When an employee starts a new job, they are required to fill out a W-4 form, which tells the employer how much tax to withhold from their paycheck. The form includes several sections, including the employee's name, address, and Social Security number, as well as information about their filing status, dependents, and any additional income or deductions that may affect their tax liability.

Calculating withholding: Based on the information provided on the W-4 form, the employer calculates the amount of tax that should be withheld from the employee's paycheck. The calculation ~~takes into account~~considers the employee's filing status, number of dependents, and any other relevant factors.

Deducting withholding from the paycheck: The employer deducts the calculated withholding amount from the employee's gross pay before issuing the paycheck. The employee receives a net pay amount, which is the amount of their paycheck after taxes have been withheld.

Remitting withholding to the government: The employer is responsible for remitting the withheld taxes to the government on behalf of the employee. The frequency of these payments depends on the size of the employer and the amount of tax withheld. Larger employers may be required to remit taxes on a more frequent basis, such as weekly or bi-weekly, while smaller employers may be able to remit taxes on a quarterly basis.

Filing a tax return: At the end of the year, the employee files a tax return with the IRS to calculate their final tax liability for the year. The tax return includes information about the employee's income, deductions, and credits, and calculates the amount of tax owed or the refund due. The amount of tax that was withheld during the year is also reported on the tax return, and is used to calculate the final tax liability.

If the amount of tax withheld during the year is greater than the final tax liability, the employee will receive a refund of the excess amount. If the amount of tax withheld is less than the final tax liability, the employee will owe additional tax when they file their return. The goal of the withholding system is to ensure that employees pay their taxes throughout the year, rather than having to come up with a large lump sum at tax time.

You may need to update your W-4 form when you get married or have children because it can affect your tax withholding. When you fill out a W-4, you are telling your employer how much money to withhold from each paycheck for federal income taxes. The amount that is withheld depends on several factors, including your filing status, number of dependents, and the amount of income you expect to earn.

When you get married or have children, your filing status may change, and you may be eligible for additional tax credits and deductions. For example, if you get married, you may be able to file jointly with your spouse, which could result in a lower tax rate and higher standard deduction. If you have children, you may be eligible for the Child Tax Credit, which can reduce your tax liability.

Updating your W-4 form can help ensure that the correct amount of taxes is being withheld from your paycheck. If you don't update your W-4 after getting married or having children, you may end up having too much or too little money withheld from your paycheck, which could result in a larger tax bill or a smaller refund when you file your tax return.

Employee vs. Freelancer

However, if you're a freelancer or self-employed, you are responsible for calculating and paying your own taxes. This means that you'll need to set aside a portion of your income to cover your tax liability. The IRS requires self-employed individuals to make quarterly estimated tax payments throughout the year, based on their projected income.

In addition, there are some key differences in the types of taxes that employees and freelancers are responsible for. As an employee, you'll typically pay income tax, Social Security tax, and Medicare tax. Your employer will also contribute to your Social Security and Medicare taxes. However, if you're a freelancer, you'll be responsible for paying the full amount of your Social Security and Medicare taxes, which is often referred to as the self-employment tax.

Another important difference between employees and freelancers is the types of tax deductions that are available to them. As an employee, you may be able to take advantage of certain deductions, such as those for unreimbursed business expenses or charitable donations. However, freelancers have access to a wider range of deductions, including deductions for home office expenses, business travel, and equipment purchases.

It's important to note that the classification of an individual as an employee or freelancer is not always straightforward. The IRS has specific guidelines for determining whether someone is an employee or an independent contractor, and misclassifying a worker can result in costly penalties for employers. If you're unsure of your classification, it's important to seek guidance from a tax professional.

Overall, understanding the differences between being an employee and a freelancer is crucial when it comes to taxes. Whether you're working for someone else or running your own business, it's important to stay informed about your tax obligations and take steps to ensure that you're meeting them in a timely and accurate manner.

Being a freelancer comes with the added responsibility of managing your own taxes. This means that you need to be proactive in setting aside a portion of your income to pay your taxes later. Unlike employees, freelancers do not have taxes withheld from their paychecks, which can be challenging for those who are new to self-employment.

One of the most important things to keep in mind as a freelancer is that you need to budget for taxes. Depending on your income level, you may be subject to a variety of taxes, including federal income tax, state income tax, self-employment tax, and possibly even local taxes. It's important to understand the tax rates and requirements that apply to your situation so that you can plan accordingly.

In addition to budgeting for taxes, freelancers may also need to make estimated tax payments throughout the year. Estimated tax payments are quarterly payments made to the IRS to cover your tax liability for the current year. These payments are based on your projected income and expenses for the year, and they are designed to help you avoid underpayment penalties. It's important to stay on top of your estimated tax payments to ensure that you're meeting your tax obligations and avoiding penalties.

Individuals who are self-employed or have income from sources that are not subject to withholding tax (such as rental income, investment income, or alimony) may be required to make estimated tax payments throughout the year to avoid underpayment penalties.

The general rule is that if you expect to owe at least $1,000 in tax for the current year after subtracting your withholding and refundable credits, you must make estimated tax payments.

For most people, estimated tax payments are due quarterly on the following dates:

April 15

June 15

September 15

January 15 of the following year

However, if any of these dates fall on a weekend or holiday, the deadline is moved to the next business day.

It's important to note that the estimated tax payments must be based on a good faith estimate of the amount of

HOW TO PAY QUARTERLY ESTIMATED TAXES

Form 1040-ES is used to pay estimated tax for income that is not subject to withholding, such as income from self-employment, rental income, and investment income. The easiest way to obtain a Form 1040-ES is to download it from the IRS website at www.irs.gov/forms.

Once on the IRS website, navigate to the Forms and Instructions section and search for Form 1040-ES. The form and instructions are available for download in both PDF and HTML formats. You can also order paper copies of the form by calling the IRS at 1-800-TAX-FORM (1-800-829-3676).

It's important to note that Form 1040-ES is not the same as Form 1040, which is the standard tax return form used to file your annual income tax return. If you need to file estimated taxes, be sure to use Form 1040-ES and follow the instructions carefully to avoid underpayment penalties.

tax that you will owe for the year. If you underpay, you may be subject to an underpayment penalty. Conversely, if you overpay, you will receive a refund when you file your tax return.

To calculate your estimated tax payments, you can use Form 1040-ES, which provides worksheets and instructions to help you estimate your tax liability for the year. You can make your payments electronically through the Electronic Federal Tax Payment System (EFTPS) or by mailing a check or money order along with the payment voucher included with Form 1040-ES.

The penalties for not paying estimated taxes vary depending on the amount of tax owed and the length of time the tax remains unpaid. Generally, if you don't pay enough tax throughout the year, either through withholding or estimated tax payments, you may be subject to a penalty.

The penalty for underpayment of estimated taxes is calculated based on the difference between the amount of tax owed and the amount of estimated tax paid, and the length of time the tax remains unpaid. The penalty is calculated for each payment period and is based on the number of days the payment is late.

The current penalty rate is determined quarterly and is based on the federal short-term rate plus 3%. As of 2021, the penalty rate is 3%.

If you fail to make estimated tax payments, you may be subject to an underpayment penalty of up to 5% of the unpaid tax for each quarter or part of a quarter in which the tax is unpaid. The penalty can be avoided if you owe less than $1,000 in tax after subtracting your withholding and refundable credits, or if you paid at least 90% of the tax for the current year or 100% of the tax shown on the previous year's return, whichever is smaller.

It's important to note that the penalty for underpayment of estimated taxes is in addition to any interest charges that may apply to unpaid taxes. To avoid penalties and interest charges, it's important to stay current with your estimated tax payments and to make sure you are paying the correct amount based on your income and deductions.

If you had no tax liability in the previous year, you may be able to waive penalties for underpayment of estimated taxes. This is known as the "prior-year safe harbor" rule. To qualify, you must have filed a tax return for the previous year and show no tax liability on that return.

To claim the waiver, you need to complete Form 2210, Underpayment of Estimated Tax by Individuals, Estates, and Trusts, and attach an explanation to the form stating that you meet the requirements for the prior-year safe harbor rule. You do not need to request the waiver specifically; the IRS will automatically apply it if you qualify.

It's important to note that the prior-year safe harbor rule only applies to penalties for underpayment of estimated taxes. If you fail to file your tax return or pay your taxes by the deadline, you may still be subject to penalties and interest charges.

Another important aspect of managing your own taxes as a freelancer is record-keeping. As a freelancer, you'll need to keep careful records of your income and expenses throughout the year to ensure that you're accurately reporting your income and taking advantage of all available deductions. This can include tracking your business-related expenses, such as office supplies, equipment, and travel expenses. You may also need to keep track of your mileage if you use your personal vehicle for business purposes.

The IRS requires taxpayers to keep accurate and complete records to support items reported on tax returns. Here are some of the general record-keeping requirements:

- ✓ Keep records that support income, deductions, and credits reported on your tax return. This includes documents such as W-2s, 1099s, receipts, invoices, and bank statements.
- ✓ Keep records for at least three years from the date you filed your original tax return or two years from the date you paid the tax, whichever is later.
- ✓ Keep records for seven years if you file a claim for a loss from worthless securities or bad debt deduction.
- ✓ Keep records indefinitely if you do not file a return, file a fraudulent return, or do not report income that you should report.
- ✓ Keep records electronically or on paper.
- ✓ Keep records in a safe place, such as a fireproof box or a secure cloud storage account.
- ✓ Keep copies of tax returns and the supporting documents used to prepare them.

Failure to keep adequate records can result in the IRS disallowing deductions, credits, and exemptions claimed on tax returns. In addition, taxpayers may be subject to penalties and interest for underpayment of taxes if they cannot provide adequate records to support their tax liabilities.

Ultimately, being a freelancer comes with unique tax responsibilities that require careful planning and organization. By budgeting for taxes, making estimated tax payments, and keeping thorough records, you can ensure that you're meeting your tax obligations and avoiding penalties. It's also a good idea to seek the advice of a tax professional to ensure that you're taking advantage of all available deductions and credits.

Your taxable income is the amount of money that you earn during a tax year that is subject to tax. Essentially, it's the amount of income that you ~~have to~~must pay taxes on. It includes not only your wages, salaries, tips, and other forms of earned income, but also income from investments such as stocks and bonds, rental properties, and business profits.

Different types of income are defined based on the source of the income and the nature of the payment. Here are some common types of income:

- ✓ Wages: Income earned through employment or self-employment.
- ✓ Tips: Income received from tips provided by customers or clients.
- ✓ Interest: Income earned from interest-bearing bank accounts or investments.
- ✓ Dividends: Income earned from investments in stocks or mutual funds.
- ✓ Capital gains: Income earned from selling investments or property for a profit.
- ✓ Rental income: Income earned from renting out property or assets.
- ✓ Business income: Income earned from owning and operating a business.
- ✓ Alimony: Income received as part of a divorce settlement or separation agreement.
- ✓ Retirement income: Income received from retirement accounts such as 401(k)s, IRAs, or pensions.
- ✓ Social Security benefits: Income received from the Social Security Administration.

18

- ✓ Unemployment compensation: Income received from state unemployment programs.
- ✓ Gambling winnings: Income earned from gambling activities, such as lottery winnings or casino jackpots.
- ✓ Scholarships and grants: Income received from academic scholarships, fellowships, or grants.

Each type of income may have its own tax implications and reporting requirements, so it's important to understand how your income is classified and how it affects your tax obligations.

However, not all income is considered taxable. Some examples of income that may be exempt from taxes include certain types of retirement income, such as Social Security benefits, and certain types of insurance payouts. Additionally, some types of income may be partially exempt, such as interest earned on municipal bonds.

To determine your taxable income, you first need to calculate your total income for the year. This includes all sources of income, including wages, self-employment income, investment income, and any other sources of income you may have. From this total, you can then subtract any deductions or credits that you are eligible for.

Many people are under the impression that you don't have to pay taxes on cash income. Alternately, plenty of people with cash income also just don't report it. Plenty of people don't report or underreport cash tips, for example. This is a bad idea on several fronts. If you don't report cash income on your tax return, you could be subject to penalties and interest charges if the IRS discovers the unreported income. Underreporting or omitting income intentionally is considered tax fraud, which is a serious offense that can result in fines and even criminal prosecution.

Beyond that, people who don't report ~~all of~~all their income are robbing themselves, and the affects will be most evident when they become older or disabled. If f you underreport your income and pay less in Social Security taxes than you ~~actually owe~~owe, you receive lower Social Security benefits in retirement. This is because your Social Security benefits are based on your lifetime earnings, which are used to calculate your Average Indexed Monthly Earnings (AIME). If your earnings are underreported, your AIME will be lower, which in turn can reduce your Social Security benefits.

if you are self-employed and underreport your income, it may impact your eligibility for Social Security benefits – including disability insurance benefits. Self-employed individuals are required to pay self-employment taxes, which fund Social Security and Medicare. If you underreport your income and pay less in self-employment taxes than you owe, you may not be earning enough credits to qualify for Social Security benefits in the future.

 If you don't report cash income on your tax return, you could be subject to penalties and interest charges if the IRS discovers the unreported income. Underreporting or omitting income intentionally is considered tax fraud, which is a serious offense that can result in fines and even criminal prosecution.

It's important to report all sources of income on your tax return, including cash income, to avoid any potential legal consequences. The IRS has various tools to identify unreported income, such as comparing the income reported on your tax return to third-party records, such as W-2s and 1099s.

If you realize that you've failed to report cash income on a previous tax return, you should file an amended return as soon as possible to correct the error and avoid additional penalties. You may also consider consulting with a tax professional to help you navigate the situation and minimize any potential legal or financial consequences.

It's important to report all sources of income on your tax return, including cash income, to avoid any potential legal consequences. The IRS has various tools to identify unreported income, such as comparing the income reported on your tax return to third-party records, such as W-2s and 1099s.

If you realize that you've failed to report cash income on a previous tax return, you should file an amended return as soon as possible to correct the error and avoid additional penalties. You may also consider consulting with a tax professional to help you navigate the situation and minimize any potential legal or financial consequences.

One of the most confusing aspect of the US tax code is the difference between deductions, exemptions and credits. To make it even worse, the 2017 Tax Cuts and Jobs Act changed the way all of it works again, so taxes don't work the way now that they did when most people were paying taxes the majority of their lives.

Deductions and exemptions are both ways to reduce your taxable income, but they are different concepts.

Deductions are expenses that you incurred during the year that the IRS allows you to subtract from your income, reducing the amount of income that is subject to taxation. Some common deductions include charitable donations, mortgage interest, state and local taxes, and medical expenses. There are two types of deductions: standard and itemized.

The standard deduction is a set amount that is subtracted from your income based on your filing status. The amount of the standard deduction changes each year and is determined by the IRS. For example, in 2021, the standard deduction for a single taxpayer is $12,900, while the standard deduction for a married couple filing jointly is $25,700.

Plenty of people think that things they used to deduct from their income are no longer deductible. That's not quite right. It's not that you can't deduct things anymore, but rather that the tax law has changed in recent years and some deductions have been eliminated or restricted. For example, the standard deduction has been increased significantly, which means that many taxpayers no longer need to itemize deductions in order to reduce their taxable income.

Additionally, the Tax Cuts and Jobs Act of 2017 eliminated or limited several deductions that were previously available. For example, the deduction for state and local taxes (SALT) is now capped at $10,000, which means that taxpayers who pay more than $10,000 in state and local taxes cannot deduct the excess amount. The deduction for unreimbursed employee expenses has also been eliminated, as has the deduction for tax preparation fees.

While some deductions have been eliminated or restricted, many others are still available. Some common deductions include charitable contributions, mortgage interest, and medical expenses. It's important to review the current tax law and consult with a tax professional to determine which deductions you may be eligible for.

Itemized deductions, on the other hand, are specific expenses that you can deduct from your income. You must list each itemized deduction on Schedule A of Form 1040 and provide proof of the expense, such as receipts or invoices. If your total itemized deductions are greater than the standard deduction, it makes sense to itemize.

Exemptions, on the other hand, are an amount that you can deduct from your income for yourself, your spouse, and each of your dependents. Prior to 2018, exemptions were a standard deduction that could be claimed by taxpayers who met certain criteria. However, the Tax Cuts and Jobs Act (TCJA) eliminated the personal exemption, and the standard deduction was increased to offset this loss. As a result, starting from 2018, taxpayers can no longer claim a personal exemption for themselves, their spouse, or their dependents.

Deductions are expenses that you can subtract from your total income to lower your taxable income. Common deductions include mortgage interest, charitable contributions, and certain business expenses, when they are higher than the standard deductions. Credits, on the other hand, are a dollar-for-dollar reduction in the amount of tax you owe. Examples of credits include the Earned Income Tax Credit, the Child Tax Credit, and the American Opportunity Tax Credit.

It's important to note that deductions and credits can vary depending on your individual circumstances. Some deductions and credits may only be available to certain groups of taxpayers, such as those who own a home or have children. It's a good idea to consult a tax professional or use tax software to ensure that you are claiming all of the deductions and credits that you are eligible for.

Tax Brackets

Understanding tax brackets is an important aspect of managing your taxes. The IRS establishes tax brackets based on your income level and filing status, and each bracket has a corresponding tax rate.

For example, for the tax year 2022, the tax brackets for a single filer are as follows:

- 10% on taxable income up to $10,275

- 12% on taxable income between $10,276 and $41,775

- 22% on taxable income between $41,776 and $89,525

- 24% on taxable income between $89,526 and $179,225

- 32% on taxable income between $179,226 and $209,425

- 35% on taxable income between $209,426 and $523,600

- 37% on taxable income over $523,600

Let's say you're a single filer with a taxable income of $50,000. You would fall into the 22% tax bracket because your taxable income falls within that range. However, only the portion of your income that falls between $41,776 and $50,000 will be taxed at that rate. The income below $41,776 will be taxed at the lower rates for those corresponding tax brackets.

It's important to note that your tax bracket is not the same as your effective tax rate. Your effective tax rate is the average rate at which your income is taxed, taking into account all of the tax brackets that apply to your income. Many people feel that when they make more money, they're being punished. It's not like that. No, going into a higher tax bracket does not mean you are being punished for making more money. Tax brackets are designed to ensure that those who earn higher incomes pay a higher percentage of their income in taxes. In the United States, the tax system is progressive, which means that as your income increases, so does the percentage of taxes you pay.

For example, let's say that the tax rate for the first $50,000 of income is 10%, and the tax rate for income between $50,001 and $100,000 is 20%. If you earn $40,000, you would pay 10% in taxes on your income. But if you earn $60,000, only the income above $50,000 ($10,000) is taxed at the higher rate of 20%, and the income below $50,000 is still taxed at the lower rate of 10%. So, your overall tax rate would be less than 20%, even though you are in a higher tax bracket.

It's also important to note that tax brackets are marginal, meaning that only the income that falls within a particular bracket is taxed at that rate. For example, if you are in the 25% tax bracket, it doesn't mean that all of your income is taxed at 25%. Only the income within that bracket is taxed at that rate, and the rest is taxed at lower rates. Your higher tax rate only applies to the percentage of your income that's inside that bracket.

Understanding tax brackets can help you plan ahead and make informed decisions about your finances. For example, if you know that you'll be in a higher tax bracket next year, you may want to consider deferring some of your income until the following year to lower your tax liability. Similarly, if you're approaching a lower tax bracket, you may want to accelerate some income into the current year to take advantage of the lower tax rate.

Conclusion

Understanding taxes is crucial for managing personal finances effectively. It is important to know the basics of taxes, such as what they are and how they work, to make informed decisions about your finances. Having a clear understanding of taxes can help you plan your budget, make smarter financial decisions, and minimize the amount you owe in taxes.

Knowing who pays taxes is essential. If you earn any form of income, you are likely required to pay taxes. This includes wages from a job, self-employment income, or income from investments. Even if you do not earn any income, you may still have to pay taxes on certain items, such as sales tax on purchases.

It is important to understand the difference between being an employee and being a freelancer. As an employee, your employer will withhold taxes from your paycheck and send them to the government on your behalf. This means that your tax liability is largely taken care of for you. However, if you are a freelancer, you are responsible for paying your own taxes. This means that you'll need to set aside a portion of your income to pay taxes later. Additionally, you may need to make estimated tax payments throughout the year to avoid penalties.

Your taxable income is the amount of money that is subject to tax. This includes wages, salaries, tips, and any other income you earn. However, not all income is taxable. For example, some types of retirement income may not be taxable, and certain deductions and credits can reduce your taxable income.

Tax brackets are another important aspect of taxes. Tax brackets refer to the ranges of income that are subject to different tax rates. The tax brackets change from year to year, but generally, the more money you make, the higher your tax rate. It is important to note that only the income within a given tax bracket is subject to that tax rate. For example, if you are in the 22% tax bracket, only the income above the previous bracket is taxed at that rate.

In addition to these basics, many factors can affect your tax liability, such as your income, deductions, and credits. In the next chapter, we'll dive deeper into deductions and credits and how they can help you reduce your tax bill. By understanding the various components of taxes, you can take control of your finances and make informed decisions to minimize the amount you owe in taxes.

Deductions and credits are two of the most important concepts to understand when it comes to managing your taxes. Both can help you lower your taxable income and reduce your overall tax bill, but they work in different ways.

Deductions are expenses that can be subtracted from your taxable income, meaning you only ~~have to~~must pay taxes on the remaining amount. Common deductions include things like mortgage interest, charitable donations, and medical expenses. The total amount of deductions you can claim depends on your filing status, income level, and other factors.

Credits, on the other hand, are dollar-for-dollar reductions in your tax bill. This means that if you have a tax credit of $1,000, your tax bill will be reduced by $1,000. Some common tax credits include the Earned Income Tax Credit, the Child Tax Credit, and the American Opportunity Tax Credit.

It's important to note that not all deductions and credits are created equal. Some are more valuable than others, depending on your individual tax situation. For example, if you are a student or have dependent children, you may qualify for credits that can significantly reduce your tax bill. Alternatively, if you own a home or have significant medical expenses, deductions may be more valuable for you.

To make the most of deductions and credits, it's important to keep good records of your expenses and consult with a tax professional if you have questions. Additionally, be sure to stay up to date on changes to the tax code, as deductions and credits can change from year to year.

By taking advantage of deductions and credits, you can lower your tax bill and keep more money in your pocket. In the next chapter, we'll explore some additional tax-saving strategies that can help you keep more of your hard-earned money.

Deductions

Deductions can come in many forms, such as business expenses, charitable donations, and even interest on certain types of loans. For example, if you are a small business owner, you can deduct expenses such as rent, utilities, and supplies. If you donate money or goods to a qualified charity, you may be able to deduct the value of your donation from your taxable income.

It's important to note that not all expenses are deductible, and there are often limits on how much you can deduct. Additionally, you may need to keep documentation to support your deductions, such as receipts or invoices. Keeping track of your expenses throughout the year can help you maximize your deductions come tax time.

One popular type of deduction is the standard deduction. This is a set amount that you can deduct from your taxable income without needing to itemize your deductions. The standard deduction amount varies depending on your filing status, and it is adjusted each year for inflation. The 2023 standard deduction is 12.900 – meaning you'd have to have more than that in deductions to itemize and benefit. Basically you'd have to spend a lot more than you probably do.

Itemizing your deductions means listing each deductible expense separately on your tax return. This can be more time-consuming than taking the standard deduction, but it can result in a lower tax bill if your total deductible expenses are greater than the standard deduction amount.

Overall, deductions can be a powerful tool for reducing your tax liability. By taking advantage of all the deductions you are eligible for, you can potentially lower your taxable income and save money on taxes. In the next section, we'll explore another way to lower your tax bill: credits.

- The standard deduction is a quick and easy way to reduce your taxable income, especially if you don't have a lot of itemized deductions to claim. However, if you do have significant expenses in certain categories, it may be worth itemizing your deductions to maximize your tax savings.

- Mortgage interest is a common itemized deduction for homeowners. If you have a mortgage on your primary residence, you can deduct the interest paid on the loan. This can be a significant deduction, especially in the early years of your mortgage when most of your payments go towards interest.

- Property taxes are another common itemized deduction for homeowners. You can deduct the amount of property taxes you paid during the year, up to a certain limit set by the IRS.

- Charitable contributions can also be deducted as itemized deductions. This includes donations to qualified organizations such as charities, churches, and educational institutions. Keep in mind that there are specific rules for deducting charitable contributions, so it's important to keep accurate records.

- Medical expenses can also be deducted as itemized deductions, but only to the extent that they exceed a certain percentage of your adjusted gross income (AGI). This threshold is currently set at 7.5% of your AGI, but it can change from year to year.

- State and local income taxes are also deductible as itemized deductions, but they are subject to a $10,000 cap. This means that if you paid more than $10,000 in state and local income taxes, you can only deduct $10,000.

- Finally, investment interest can also be deducted as an itemized deduction. This includes interest paid on loans used to purchase investments such as stocks or mutual funds. However, there are limits to how much investment interest you can deduct each year.

- It's important to note that not all expenses can be deducted. For example, personal expenses such as groceries, clothing, and transportation are not deductible. Additionally, some deductions are subject to certain limitations or phase-outs based on your income or other factors. It's always a good idea to consult with a tax professional or use tax preparation software to ensure you are maximizing your deductions while staying within the rules.

Deductions can have different rules and limitations depending on the type of expense and your income level. For example, the deduction for state and local taxes (SALT) has a $10,000 cap. This means that you can only deduct up to $10,000 in combined state and local income, property, and sales taxes. Additionally, some deductions may be subject to phase-outs based on your income level. For example, the deduction for traditional IRA contributions is phased out for those with high incomes who also have access to a retirement plan at work.

It's also important to understand that if you choose to take the standard deduction, you cannot itemize deductions. This means that you cannot deduct specific expenses like mortgage interest, property taxes, and charitable contributions. In some cases, the standard deduction may be more beneficial for you than itemizing deductions. You should always calculate both options to determine which one will result in the lower tax bill.

Credits

Tax credits are a powerful tool to lower your tax bill and increase your tax refund. They are often more valuable than deductions because they provide a dollar-for-dollar reduction in your tax liability. There are two main types of tax credits: refundable and non-refundable.

A refundable tax credit is a credit that can reduce your tax liability below zero, meaning you can receive a refund for the remaining amount. For example, if you owe $2,000 in taxes but have a refundable credit of $2,500, you would not only eliminate your tax liability but also receive a $500 refund. Common examples of refundable tax credits include the Earned Income Tax Credit (EITC) and the Child Tax Credit.

non-refundable tax credits, on the other hand, can only reduce your tax liability to zero. If the credit exceeds your tax liability, you will not receive a refund for the difference. For example, if you owe $2,000 in taxes but have a non-refundable credit of $3,000, you would only be able to reduce your tax liability to zero and not receive any refund for the remaining $1,000. Some common non-refundable tax credits include the Lifetime Learning Credit and the Retirement Savings Contributions Credit.

It's important to note that some tax credits have income limits, meaning they are only available to individuals or families with certain income levels. Additionally, some tax credits are available only for specific expenses, such as the Child and Dependent Care Credit for child care expenses or the Adoption Credit for adoption-related expenses.

Education credits are a type of tax credit that can help offset the costs of higher education for you or your dependents. These credits are available to eligible taxpayers who have incurred qualifying expenses related to higher education.

There are two main education credits: the American Opportunity Tax Credit (AOTC) and the Lifetime Learning Credit (LLC). The AOTC is more generous and is available to eligible students for up to four years of undergraduate study. The LLC, on the other hand, can be claimed for an unlimited number of years and can be used for undergraduate or graduate studies, as well as for job training courses.

The American Opportunity Tax Credit (AOTC): This credit is available for the first four years of post-secondary education and can be worth up to $2,500 per student per year. To qualify, the student must be enrolled at least half-time in a degree or certificate program and must not have completed their fourth year of post-secondary education.

The Lifetime Learning Credit (LLC): This credit is available for all years of post-secondary education and can be worth up to $2,000 per tax return. Unlike the AOTC, there is no limit on the number of years this credit can be claimed. To qualify, the student must be enrolled in at least one course at an eligible educational institution.

To be eligible for education credits, you or your dependent must have been enrolled at an eligible educational institution for at least one academic period during the tax year. You must also meet certain income limits and other criteria.

percentage of these expenses and can reduce the amount of tax you owe dollar-for-dollar.

It's important to note that education credits are subject to phase-out limits and income limits. This means that as your income increases, the amount of the credit you are eligible for will decrease until it is phased out completely.

Overall, education credits can be a valuable way to help offset the costs of higher education, but it's important to understand the eligibility requirements and limitations before claiming them on your tax return.

The child tax credit is a tax credit offered by the IRS to parents or guardians of qualifying children under the age of 17. The credit reduces the amount of taxes owed by the taxpayer on a dollar-for-dollar basis. The maximum amount of the credit is $2,000 per qualifying child, and up to $1,400 of that amount can be refundable.

To qualify for the child tax credit, the child must be a U.S. citizen, U.S. national, or resident alien, and have a valid Social Security number. Additionally, the child must have lived with the taxpayer for more than half of the year and must be claimed as a dependent on the taxpayer's tax return.

There are income limitations to be eligible for the full child tax credit amount. As of 2021, the credit begins to phase out for single filers with incomes over $200,000, and for married couples filing jointly with incomes over $400,000.

The child tax credit can also be partially refundable, meaning that if the credit reduces the taxpayer's liability below zero, the taxpayer may receive a refund of up to $1,400 per child.

The credit is subject to certain phase-out limitations based on income. .]+/01

The amount of the education credit is based on the qualified education expenses paid during

the tax year, including tuition, fees, and required course materials. The credit is calculated as a

The Earned Income Tax Credit (EITC) is a tax credit designed to provide financial support to low- and moderate-income workers. The credit is based on earned income and is intended to help individuals and families who earn below a certain income level.

The credit can be quite substantial for eligible individuals and families, potentially providing thousands of dollars in tax relief. To qualify for the EITC, you must meet certain eligibility requirements, including having earned income, filing a tax return, and meeting certain income limits.

The amount of the credit is based on your earned income and the number of qualifying children in your household. The credit phases out as income increases, and the amount of the credit varies depending on your filing status and income level.

One of the unique features of the EITC is that it is a refundable credit, which means that if the credit is more than the taxes owed, the excess credit will be refunded to the taxpayer. This can be especially helpful for low-income families who may be struggling to make ends meet.

It's important to note that there are some restrictions on who can claim the EITC. For example, if you are married filing separately, you are not eligible for the credit. Additionally, if you have investment income above a certain threshold, you may not be eligible for the credit.

Overall, the EITC is an important tax credit that can provide valuable financial support to low- and moderate-income workers. If you think you may be eligible for the credit, it's important to speak with a tax professional or use tax software to ensure that you claim the credit correctly on your tax return.

Overall, tax credits can be a valuable tool to reduce your tax liability and keep more money in

your pocket. Make sure to research the different tax credits available to you and consult with a

tax professional to see which ones you qualify for and how to claim them on your tax return.

Tax credits are a valuable tool for taxpayers to lower their tax bill. The child tax credit is a

common credit that can provide significant savings for families with children under the age of

17. The maximum credit amount is $2,000 per child and is subject to income limits. The earned income tax credit (EITC) is another credit designed to help low to moderate-income workers. The credit amount is based on your earned income and the number of children you have, and it can be worth up to $6,728 in 2021.

Education credits, such as the American Opportunity Credit and the Lifetime Learning Credit, can help offset the cost of higher education. These credits can be used to cover expenses such as tuition, fees, and textbooks, and are subject to income limits.

The Retirement Savings Contributions Credit, also known as the Saver's Credit, is a credit designed to encourage low to moderate-income taxpayers to save for retirement. The credit is based on the amount of money you contribute to a qualifying retirement account, such as a 401(k) or IRA.

The Health Insurance Premium Tax Credit is a credit available to help offset the cost of health insurance for those who purchase insurance through the Health Insurance Marketplace. This credit is based on your income and the cost of the insurance plan you choose.

It's important to note that some tax credits are refundable, while others are not. A refundable credit, such as the EITC, can provide a refund even if you don't owe any taxes. In contrast, a non-refundable credit can only reduce your tax liability to zero, but cannot provide a refund.

Like deductions, tax credits also have restrictions and income limits that can affect your eligibility. It's important to understand the requirements and restrictions of each credit to ensure that you are taking advantage of all the tax credits you are eligible for.

Maximizing Your Tax Savings

To begin, it's important to have a solid understanding of the deductions and credits that are available to you. As mentioned earlier, there are two types of deductions: standard and itemized. The standard deduction is a fixed amount that varies based on your filing status, while itemized deductions are specific expenses that can be deducted if they exceed the standard deduction amount. Keeping track of these expenses throughout the year can help ensure that you maximize your tax savings.

Similarly, understanding the various tax credits available to you is crucial for maximizing your savings. This involves knowing the eligibility requirements, income limits, and the specific expenses that can be used to qualify for each credit. By knowing the ins and outs of each credit, you can ensure that you are taking full advantage of the credits you are eligible for.

To keep track of your expenses, it's important to maintain accurate and detailed records throughout the year. This may involve keeping receipts for deductible expenses like charitable donations, medical expenses, and business expenses. It's also important to stay informed about any changes to the tax code that may impact your eligibility for certain deductions and credits.

Another important step in maximizing your tax savings is working with a qualified tax professional. A tax professional can provide guidance on which deductions and credits you qualify for and can help ensure that you are taking full advantage of all available tax breaks.

Finally, it's important to plan ahead when it comes to taxes. This involves estimating your tax liability early on in the year and making adjustments to your income and expenses as needed to minimize your tax bill. By taking proactive steps to maximize your tax savings throughout the year, you can reduce the stress and financial burden of tax season.

Working with a tax professional can provide a number of benefits when it comes to maximizing your tax savings. Tax professionals are trained and experienced in navigating the complex tax code and can help you identify deductions and credits that you may not have been aware of. They can also provide guidance on tax planning strategies that can help you reduce your tax liability.

In addition to tax professionals, there are also a variety of tax software programs available that can help you prepare and file your taxes. These programs can be a cost-effective alternative to hiring a tax professional, and they often provide step-by-step guidance and tools to help you identify deductions and credits.

When using tax software, it's important to choose a reputable program and to carefully review your return for accuracy. While tax software can be a helpful tool, it's still important to understand the tax code and the deductions and credits you are claiming.

Ultimately, whether you choose to work with a tax professional or use tax software, being proactive and staying informed about changes to the tax code can help you maximize your tax savings and keep more money in your pocket.

Conclusion

Tax planning strategies for small business owners involve understanding the unique tax rules and regulations that apply to businesses. By taking advantage of deductions and credits, as well as implementing tax planning strategies, small business owners can reduce their tax liability and keep more money in their business.

One tax planning strategy for small business owners is to consider the type of business entity they have. For example, a sole proprietorship may be subject to different tax rules than a partnership or corporation. Understanding the tax implications of each type of entity can help small business owners choose the best option for their business.

Another tax planning strategy is to keep careful records of all business expenses throughout the year. This can include expenses such as office supplies, travel expenses, and equipment purchases. By keeping accurate records, small business owners can take advantage of deductions and credits that apply to their specific industry.

Small business owners can also consider making contributions to retirement accounts, such as a Simplified Employee Pension (SEP) or a 401(k) plan. These contributions can provide tax savings and help small business owners save for retirement.

Additionally, small business owners can take advantage of the Section 179 deduction, which allows businesses to deduct the full cost of qualifying equipment purchases in the year they are made. This deduction can be particularly beneficial for small businesses that need to purchase expensive equipment.

It's important for small business owners to work with a tax professional to ensure that they are taking advantage of all the deductions and credits available to them. A tax professional can also help small business owners create a tax plan that meets their unique needs and goals. By implementing tax planning strategies and taking advantage of deductions and credits, small business owners can reduce their tax liability and keep more money in their business.

Chapter 3: Tax Planning Strategies for Small Business Owners

As a small business owner, taxes are an essential aspect of your financial planning. Proper tax planning can help you to minimize your tax liability, keep more of your profits, and avoid any potential penalties from the IRS. Here are some strategies that you can consider to reduce your tax bill:

1. Keep Accurate Records: Accurate and organized record-keeping is essential for all businesses. Keep track of all your expenses, including receipts, invoices, and bank statements, so that you can easily identify any eligible deductions.

2. Take Advantage of Deductions: Small business owners are eligible for many tax deductions, such as expenses for equipment, travel, advertising, and office space. Deductions can help reduce your taxable income, which can lower your tax bill.

3. Consider a Retirement Plan: Retirement plans such as a Simplified Employee Pension (SEP) or Individual Retirement Account (IRA) offer tax advantages to small business owners. Contributions made to a retirement plan are tax-deductible and can lower your taxable income.

4. Hire Family Members: Hiring family members can provide tax benefits. For example, you can deduct their salaries as business expenses, and your family members can contribute to a retirement plan.

5. Use a Home Office Deduction: If you use part of your home for business purposes, you may be able to claim a home office deduction. This deduction allows you to deduct a portion of your home expenses, such as utilities, mortgage interest, and property taxes.

6. Choose the Right Business Entity: The type of business entity you choose can significantly affect your tax liability. Consider the tax implications of each entity, such as a sole proprietorship, partnership, or corporation, and choose the one that offers the most tax benefits.

7. Hire a Tax Professional: A tax professional can help you navigate the complex tax laws, identify eligible deductions, and create a tax plan that maximizes your savings.

By following these tax planning strategies, you can reduce your tax bill and keep more of your hard-earned money. It's essential to stay informed about the latest tax laws and regulations, so you can take advantage of any new opportunities to minimize your tax liability.

Understand Your Business Structure

A sole proprietorship is the simplest and most common type of business structure. As the sole owner of the business, you report all business income and expenses on your personal tax return, using a Schedule C form. This means that your business income is subject to both income tax and self-employment tax, which covers Social Security and Medicare taxes for self-employed individuals.

In a partnership, two or more owners share ownership and responsibility for the business. Partnerships are also pass-through entities, meaning that the business income and expenses are reported on each partner's personal tax return, using a Schedule K-1 form. Like sole proprietorships, partnerships are subject to income tax and self-employment tax.

Limited liability companies (LLCs) are a popular choice for small business owners because they offer the limited liability protection of a corporation while still being taxed as a pass-through entity. This means that the business income and expenses are reported on the owner's personal tax return, using a Schedule C or Schedule K-1 form. LLCs can also choose to be taxed as a corporation, which can have different tax implications.

Corporations are separate legal entities from their owners, meaning that the corporation pays its own taxes and is subject to corporate income tax. Owners of a corporation, known as shareholders, report any dividends they receive on their personal tax return. Corporations are also subject to double taxation, meaning that the corporation pays taxes on its income and the shareholders pay taxes on any dividends they receive.

Choosing the right business structure can have a significant impact on your tax liability, so it's important to consider the pros and cons of each structure and consult with a tax professional before ~~making a decision~~deciding.

Take Advantage of Deductions

Home office expenses refer to the costs associated with maintaining a designated space in your home that is used exclusively for business purposes. This deduction can include expenses such as rent, utilities, and internet service, but only for the percentage of your home that is used for your business. To qualify for this deduction, your home office must be your principal place of business, and you must use it regularly and exclusively for business purposes.

Business travel expenses refer to the costs associated with traveling for business purposes, such as airfare, lodging, meals, and transportation. To qualify for this deduction, the travel must be necessary and directly related to your business. Additionally, you must keep detailed records of your travel expenses, including receipts and the purpose of the trip.

Equipment and supply expenses refer to the costs associated with purchasing or leasing equipment and supplies necessary for your business, such as computers, office furniture, and office supplies. These expenses can be deducted in the year they are incurred or depreciated over several years, depending on the type of equipment.

Vehicle expenses refer to the costs associated with using a vehicle for business purposes, such as gas, oil changes, repairs, and depreciation. To qualify for this deduction, you must keep detailed records of your mileage and the purpose of each trip.

Health insurance premiums can also be deducted by small business owners who pay for their own health insurance or for the health insurance of their employees. This deduction can be taken on the business's tax return, reducing the business's taxable income.

It's important to keep accurate and detailed records of all your expenses throughout the year to ensure that you are taking advantage of all the deductions you are eligible for. By tracking your expenses, you can minimize your tax liability and keep more of your hard-earned money.

Plan Your Retirement Contributions

A solo 401(k), also known as an individual 401(k), is a retirement plan designed for self-employed individuals or business owners with no employees, other than a spouse. It operates similarly to a traditional 401(k) plan offered by larger companies, but with some additional benefits for small business owners.

With a solo 401(k), you can make contributions as both an employee and an employer. As an employee, you can contribute up to 100% of your income, up to a maximum of $19,500 in 2021. As an employer, you can contribute up to 25% of your net income, up to a maximum of $58,000 in 2021. This allows you to potentially save more for retirement than with other retirement plans.

A Simplified Employee Pension (SEP) plan is another retirement plan option for small business owners. With a SEP plan, you can contribute up to 25% of your net income, up to a maximum of $58,000 in 2021. Unlike a solo 401(k), you cannot make employee contributions to a SEP plan, but you can make contributions on behalf of your employees if you have any.

Both a solo 401(k) and a SEP plan offer tax benefits by allowing contributions to be made with pre-tax dollars, reducing your taxable income. Additionally, earnings on the investments within the account are tax-deferred, meaning you don't pay taxes on the earnings until you withdraw the money in retirement.

It's important to consider the pros and cons of each retirement plan option and consult with a tax professional to determine which plan is best for your business and retirement goals.

Consult with a Tax Professional

Working with a tax professional can provide numerous benefits for small business owners. Tax professionals are knowledgeable about tax laws and regulations and can help small business owners navigate the complex tax code. They can help you identify deductions and credits that you may not have been aware of, and ensure that you are in compliance with all tax laws and regulations.

In addition to helping you reduce your tax liability, a tax professional can also help you with tax planning strategies for the future. They can help you plan for retirement, make decisions about investments and assets, and ensure that you are taking advantage of all available tax benefits. They can also help you plan for major business events, such as mergers or acquisitions, and ensure that you are not caught off guard by unexpected tax consequences.

Furthermore, a tax professional can provide peace of mind for small business owners by ensuring that all tax filings are accurate and on time. This can help you avoid costly penalties and fines, as well as any legal repercussions that may result from noncompliance with tax laws.

Overall, consulting with a tax professional is an important part of tax planning for small business owners. By working with a professional, you can ensure that you are taking advantage of all available tax benefits and planning for the future in a tax-efficient manner.

Conclusion

Tax planning strategies are not limited to small business owners, and individuals and families can also benefit from taking proactive steps to reduce their tax liability. By understanding the tax code and being aware of the deductions and credits available to them, individuals and families can save significant amounts of money on their taxes.

One of the first things to consider when planning your taxes as an individual or family is your filing status. Your filing status can affect your tax liability, so it's important to understand the different options available and choose the one that best fits your situation. For example, married couples can choose to file jointly or separately, and each option has its own tax implications.

Another key tax planning strategy is to take advantage of deductions and credits. Common deductions for individuals and families include charitable donations, mortgage interest, and state and local taxes. Credits, such as the Earned Income Tax Credit and the Child Tax Credit, can also provide significant tax savings.

Contributing to a retirement account, such as an Individual Retirement Account (IRA) or a 401(k), can also be a powerful tax planning tool for individuals and families. These contributions can reduce your taxable income and help you save for retirement at the same time.

Working with a tax professional can also be beneficial for individuals and families. A tax professional can help you navigate the tax code, identify areas where you can save money on your taxes, and ensure that you are in compliance with follow all tax laws and regulations.

In summary, tax planning strategies are not just for small business owners. Individuals and families can also benefit from understanding the tax code, taking advantage of deductions and credits, planning their retirement contributions, and working with a tax professional.

Chapter 4: Tax Planning Strategies for Individuals and Families

As an individual or family, there are several tax planning strategies that you can use to reduce your tax liability and keep more of your money. One of the first things you can do is to take advantage of deductions and credits that you are eligible for. Some common deductions and credits include:

1. Charitable donations: Donations made to qualified charitable organizations can be tax-deductible, meaning you can reduce your taxable income by the amount you donated.

2. Retirement contributions: Contributing to a retirement account, such as a traditional IRA or a 401(k), can help you reduce your taxable income and save for the future.

3. Education expenses: If you or your dependents are enrolled in higher education, you may be eligible for tax credits or deductions for tuition and other education-related expenses.

4. Health care expenses: If you have high medical expenses, you may be able to deduct them on your taxes.

5. Homeownership expenses: If you own a home, you may be able to deduct mortgage interest and property taxes on your taxes.

It's important to keep detailed records of your expenses throughout the year to ensure that you are taking advantage of all the deductions and credits you are eligible for.

Another tax planning strategy for individuals and families is to consider your tax filing status. Your filing status can affect your tax liability, so it's important to choose the one that works best for your situation. For example, if you're married, you may choose to file jointly or separately depending on your income and other factors.

Finally, working with a tax professional can be a valuable tax planning strategy for individuals and families. A tax professional can help you navigate the tax code, identify areas where you can save money on your taxes, and ensure that you ~~are in compliance with~~are following all tax laws and regulations.

Take Advantage of Tax-Advantaged Accounts

One of the best ways to reduce your taxable income and save for the future is to take advantage of tax-advantaged accounts. There are several types of tax-advantaged accounts available, such as:

- Individual Retirement Accounts (IRAs)
- 401(k) plans
- Health Savings Accounts (HSAs)
- 529 college savings plans

These accounts allow you to contribute pre-tax dollars, which reduces your taxable income and helps you save for the future. Additionally, some accounts, such as HSAs and 529 plans, offer tax-free withdrawals for qualified expenses.

Be Mindful of Your Investment Choices

When it comes to investing, it's important to consider the tax implications of your choices. By being strategic with your investments, you can reduce your tax liability and keep more of your returns.

One way to minimize your taxes on investments is to hold stocks for more than a year before selling them. This allows you to take advantage of lower long-term capital gains tax rates, which can be significantly lower than short-term capital gains rates. This means that you can potentially keep more of your profits by holding onto your investments for a longer ~~period of time~~period.

Another way to reduce your tax liability on investments is to invest in tax-exempt or tax-deferred accounts. Municipal bonds, for example, are typically exempt from federal income tax and may also be exempt from state and local taxes if you invest in bonds issued by your state or municipality. Annuities, on the other hand, allow you to defer taxes on your investment earnings until you start making withdrawals, potentially allowing you to withdraw the funds when you're in a lower tax bracket.

It's important to note that not all investments are created equal when it comes to taxes, and the tax implications can vary depending on your individual circumstances. Working with a financial advisor or tax professional can help you make informed decisions about your investments and ensure that you're maximizing your tax savings.

Maximize Your Deductions and Credits

Charitable donations are a popular deduction for individuals and families who give to non-profit organizations. These donations can include cash donations, as well as donations of goods and property. It's important to keep track of these donations throughout the year and obtain a receipt or acknowledgment letter from the organization to prove the donation for tax purposes.

Mortgage interest is another common deduction for homeowners. The interest paid on a mortgage is deductible up to a certain amount, depending on the type of mortgage and the value of the home. This deduction can provide significant tax savings for homeowners.

State and local taxes, or SALT, can also be deducted on your federal tax return. This includes state income tax, property tax, and sales tax. However, the deduction for state and local taxes is limited to $10,000 per year under current tax law.

Child tax credits and education credits are available to help families with children. The child tax credit can provide a credit of up to $2,000 per qualifying child, while education credits can provide a credit for tuition and education-related expenses. These credits can help offset the costs of raising a family and provide significant tax savings.

It's important to keep track of all ofall your expenses throughout the year and consult with a tax professional to ensure that you are taking advantage of all the deductions and credits available to you. By doing so, you can reduce your tax liability and keep more of your hard-earned money.

Consider a Roth Conversion

A Roth conversion is a strategy that can be used by individuals who have a traditional IRA or 401(k) plan and want to reduce their future tax liability. When you contribute to a traditional IRA or 401(k) plan, you do so with pre-tax dollars, meaning that you receive a tax deduction in the year of contribution. However, when you withdraw money from a traditional account in retirement, you will have to pay taxes on the withdrawals at your ordinary income tax rate.

With a Roth conversion, you can transfer funds from a traditional account to a Roth account. The funds that are transferred will be subject to income tax in the year of the conversion, but after that, the funds in the Roth account can grow tax-free and be withdrawn tax-free in retirement. This can be a powerful tool for reducing your future tax liability and maximizing your retirement savings.

However, it's important to note that Roth conversions can be complex and have tax implications. For example, the income from the conversion may push you into a higher tax bracket, resulting in a larger tax bill. Additionally, if you are under age 59 and a half, you may be subject to a 10% early withdrawal penalty on the amount converted.

Therefore, it's important to consult with a tax professional before making a Roth conversion. They can help you evaluate your individual tax situation and determine if a Roth conversion is the right strategy for you.

Conclusion

Tax planning strategies are important for individuals and families to reduce their tax liability and maximize their financial security. One of the most effective ways to do this is by taking advantage of tax-advantaged accounts such as IRAs, 401(k) plans, HSAs, and 529 college savings plans. These accounts can help reduce taxable income, grow tax-free or tax-deferred, and provide tax-free withdrawals for qualified expenses.

Investment choices can also impact your tax liability. It's important to be mindful of the tax implications of investments, such as capital gains tax rates, and to consider investing in tax-exempt or tax-deferred accounts.

Maximizing deductions and credits is another way to reduce your tax liability. Charitable donations, mortgage interest, state and local taxes, child tax credits, and education credits are just a few examples of deductions and credits that can help lower your tax bill. Keeping detailed records of your expenses is essential to ensure that you are claiming all the deductions and credits you are eligible for.

Finally, a Roth conversion can be a powerful tax planning strategy for individuals and families. By converting funds from a traditional account to a Roth account, you can potentially avoid taxes on those funds in retirement. However, it's important to consult with a tax professional before making a Roth conversion, as there may be tax implications and other factors to consider.

When it comes to selecting a tax professional, it's important to consider qualifications, reputation, fees, and communication. A qualified and reputable tax professional can help you navigate the complex world of taxes and provide peace of mind during tax season.

Despite the importance of tax planning, many individuals and families make common tax mistakes that can result in unnecessary tax liability. In the next chapter, we'll explore some of these common mistakes and how to avoid them.

Chapter 5: Common Tax Mistakes to Avoid

One of the most common tax mistakes is failing to file or pay taxes on time. If you miss the tax filing deadline or fail to pay the taxes you owe, you may face penalties and interest charges. To avoid this mistake, it's important to stay organized and keep track of important tax deadlines throughout the year. You can also consider setting up automatic payments or reminders to help ensure that you file and pay on time.

Another common tax mistake is making errors on your tax return. This can include mistakes in math, incorrect or incomplete information, and failing to report all of your income. To avoid this mistake, it's important to double-check your tax return before submitting it and to ensure that you have all the necessary documentation to support your claims.

Failing to take advantage of all the tax deductions and credits you are eligible for is another common tax mistake. This can lead to paying more in taxes than necessary. To avoid this mistake, it's important to research and understand the deductions and credits available to you, and to keep detailed records of your expenses throughout the year.

Finally, failing to seek professional advice or guidance when filing your taxes can also be a costly mistake. A tax professional can help ensure that you are taking advantage of all the tax planning strategies available to you and can help you avoid making costly mistakes. By working with a qualified and reputable tax professional, you can feel more confident in your tax filings and reduce the risk of penalties, interest, and other financial consequences.

Filing Late or Not at All

Late or non-filing of tax returns is a common mistake that can lead to a variety of negative consequences. If you file your taxes late or not at all, you could face penalties and interest charges, which can add up quickly and increase your tax bill. Additionally, the IRS may take enforcement action, such as wage garnishment or property liens, to collect the taxes owed.

To avoid this mistake, it's important to make sure you file your tax return on time. The deadline for filing individual tax returns is usually April 15th, but it may be extended in certain situations, such as a natural disaster or pandemic-related relief. If you are unable to pay your full tax liability by the deadline, you should still file your tax return on time and then explore payment options, such as an installment agreement with the IRS.

Another way to avoid late or non-filing of tax returns is to be organized and keep accurate records of your income and expenses throughout the year. This can help ensure that you have all the necessary information to file your tax return on time and accurately.

In addition, it's important to seek help from a tax professional if you are struggling to file your taxes or pay your tax bill. A tax professional can provide guidance on available options for resolving tax issues and help you avoid penalties and interest charges.

Not Reporting All Income

Inaccurate reporting of income is a common mistake made by taxpayers, which can lead to significant financial consequences. It is important to understand that all sources of income are taxable, including wages, salaries, tips, interest, dividends, capital gains, and other sources. If you fail to report ~~all of~~all your income, the IRS may identify the discrepancy through their matching program and send you a notice of deficiency, which can result in penalties and interest charges.

To avoid this mistake, keep accurate and detailed records of all of your income throughout the year. This includes income from freelance work, side gigs, and any other sources of income. When filing your taxes, double-check your W-2 and 1099 forms to ensure that they accurately reflect your income for the year. If you realize that you have not reported all of your income, file an amended tax return as soon as possible to avoid any further penalties and interest charges.

Being upfront and honest about all of your income is crucial in avoiding potential legal and financial issues with the IRS. Always consult with a tax professional if you have any doubts or questions regarding your income reporting.

Forgetting Deductions and Credits

It's important to remember that deductions and credits can significantly reduce your tax liability, so it's crucial to take advantage of them. Charitable donations, mortgage interest, and education credits are just a few examples of deductions and credits that can save you money on your taxes.

One way to make sure you're not missing out on any deductions or credits is to keep detailed records of your expenses throughout the year. This can include receipts, invoices, and bank statements. By doing so, you'll be able to accurately track your expenses and ensure that you're claiming all the deductions you're entitled to.

Another way to maximize your deductions and credits is to work with a tax professional. A qualified tax professional can help you identify all the deductions and credits you're eligible for and ensure that you're claiming them correctly on your tax return. They can also provide valuable advice on tax planning strategies that can help you reduce your tax liability in the future.

Overall, it's important to be proactive about maximizing your deductions and credits. By keeping accurate records and working with a tax professional, you can avoid this common tax mistake and reduce your tax liability.

Not understanding Who counts for Tax Credits

In general, you cannot claim someone else's child as your dependent on your tax return unless you have a qualifying relationship with the child and meet certain criteria. The IRS has strict

CLAIMING CHILDREN AS DEPENDANTS

This is one area that the IRS scrutinizes, especially if you're claiming a child that is not your biological child. Now don't take this as not being able to claim a child you ~~actually support~~support. I see clients all the time who have custody of grandchildren, nieces and nephews – and in one instance a woman who was raising her five great-grandchildren.

You absolutely should claim children for whom you provide support. But be aware you will need to simply show documentation to back up the fact that you are declaring you provide support for that child.

rules about who can claim a child as a dependent, and these rules are in place to prevent multiple people from claiming the same child and receiving tax benefits for that child.

To claim someone else's child as a dependent, you must have legal custody or guardianship of the child, or the child must have lived with you for more than half of the year and meet the other qualifying child tests, such as age and relationship. If you do not have legal custody or guardianship, you may still be able to claim the child if the custodial parent or legal guardian agrees to sign a written declaration giving up their right to claim the child as a dependent.

It is important to note that claiming someone else's child as a dependent when you do not have the legal right to do so can result in penalties and even criminal charges for tax fraud. It is important to follow the IRS rules and only claim dependents that you are legally entitled to claim.

Not Double-Checking Your Return

Reviewing your tax return carefully is a crucial step to avoid common tax mistakes. Before submitting your return, double-check for any errors or omissions that could lead to penalties or delays in processing. This includes ensuring that all information, such as Social Security numbers, names, and addresses, are correct and up-to-date.

It's also important to review your math calculations and make sure all of your income and deductions are accurately reported. A small math error could cause your tax liability to be incorrect, which could lead to penalties and interest charges.

To avoid this mistake, take the time to review your tax return carefully before submitting it. Consider using tax software or hiring a tax professional to help you prepare your return and ensure that all calculations are correct. Additionally, consider having a trusted friend or family member review your return to catch any mistakes that you might have missed.

By taking the time to review your return for errors and omissions, you can help ensure that your return is processed correctly and avoid any unnecessary penalties or interest charges.

Conclusion

Filing taxes can be a daunting task for many individuals and families. However, by avoiding common tax mistakes, taxpayers can avoid penalties, interest charges, and audits by the IRS. One of the most common mistakes is filing taxes late or not filing at all. Taxpayers who fail to file their taxes on time can face a penalty that could add up to 5% of their unpaid taxes for each month they're late, up to 25% of the total amount owed. This can be a costly mistake that can easily be avoided by filing on time.

Another common mistake is failing to report all of your income on your tax return. This can include income from freelance work, side gigs, and other sources. Taxpayers who fail to report all of their income can be penalized and even audited by the IRS. To avoid this mistake, it's important to keep accurate records of all your income and report it on your tax return.

Additionally, many taxpayers miss out on valuable deductions and credits that can significantly reduce their tax liability. Common deductions and credits include charitable donations, mortgage interest, and education credits. Taxpayers who fail to take advantage of these deductions and credits can end up paying more in taxes than necessary. To avoid this mistake, it's important to keep detailed records of your expenses and consult with a tax professional to ensure you're taking advantage of all the deductions and credits you're eligible for.

Before submitting your tax return, it's also important to double-check for errors and omissions. Even small mistakes, such as incorrect Social Security numbers or math errors, can lead to delays and penalties. To avoid this mistake, taxpayers should review their returns carefully and consider having a tax professional or trusted friend or family member review it as well.

In summary, avoiding common tax mistakes can save taxpayers from unnecessary financial burdens and complications. By filing taxes on time, reporting all of your income, taking advantage of deductions and credits, and double-checking your return, you can ensure a smooth and hassle-free tax filing process. In the next chapter, we'll explore tips for selecting a tax professional to help you with your taxes.

Enrolled Agents

Enrolled Agents, or EAs, are tax professionals who are licensed by the IRS. They are authorized to represent taxpayers before the IRS for tax issues, including audits, collections, and appeals. EAs must pass a comprehensive exam that covers individual and business tax returns, and they must also meet ongoing education requirements to maintain their license.

EAs specialize in taxation and can provide tax preparation, tax planning, and representation services to individuals and businesses. They can also provide guidance on complex tax issues, such as estate and trust taxes, and international taxation.

Tax Attorneys

Tax attorneys are lawyers who specialize in tax law. They have earned a law degree and have passed a state bar exam. Tax attorneys can provide legal advice on a wide range of tax issues, including tax disputes, audits, and appeals.

Tax attorneys can also provide tax planning and preparation services, although they may focus more on complex tax issues and representation in tax court. They can also provide guidance on estate planning, business structuring, and other legal issues related to taxation.

Choosing a Tax Professional

When selecting a tax professional, it's important to consider their qualifications, experience, reputation, fees, and communication. Here are some tips to help you choose a tax professional:

- Check their qualifications: Look for a tax professional who is licensed and has the appropriate credentials, such as a CPA, EA, or tax attorney.
- Consider their experience: Look for a tax professional who has experience working with individuals and families in your specific tax situation.
- Check their reputation: Look for reviews and references from other clients, and check with the Better Business Bureau or state licensing boards for any complaints or disciplinary actions.
- Consider their fees: Look for a tax professional who charges reasonable fees and is transparent about their pricing structure.
- Evaluate their communication: Look for a tax professional who communicates clearly and promptly, and who is willing to answer your questions and explain complex tax issues in understandable terms.

By following these tips and choosing a qualified and reputable tax professional, you can ensure that you receive expert guidance and advice on your taxes, and can avoid common tax mistakes that can lead to penalties and other financial consequences.

In addition to their legal expertise, tax attorneys can also provide tax preparation and planning services. However, they typically focus on more complex tax issues and may be more expensive than other types of tax professionals.

Choosing the Right Tax Professional When selecting a tax professional, it's important to consider their qualifications, experience, and reputation. Here are some tips to help you choose the right tax professional:

- ✓ Consider their qualifications: Make sure the tax professional you choose has the appropriate licenses and certifications for their field.
- ✓ Look for experience: Ask about the tax professional's experience in working with clients in situations similar to yours.
- ✓ Check their reputation: Read reviews and ask for referrals from friends and family. Look for a tax professional with a solid reputation in the community.
- ✓ Consider their fees: Make sure you understand the tax professional's fee structure and that it fits within your budget.
- ✓ Assess their communication skills: Make sure you feel comfortable communicating with the tax professional and that they are responsive to your needs.

By considering these factors and asking the right questions, you can find a tax professional who can assist you with your taxes and provide peace of mind during tax season.

Choosing a Tax Professional

Qualifications and expertise are essential factors to consider when choosing a tax professional. You want to make sure that the professional you choose has the necessary qualifications, education, and experience in the specific area of taxes that you need help with. For example, if you own a small business, you may want to look for a tax professional who has expertise in small business taxes.

Reputation is another important factor to consider when selecting a tax professional. You can check reviews and references to see what other clients have said about their experience with the professional. You can also ask for recommendations from friends, family, or colleagues who have used a tax professional in the past.

Fees are another crucial factor to consider. Make sure to understand the fees upfront and what services are included. Some tax professionals may charge a flat fee, while others may charge an hourly rate. Be wary of tax professionals who charge a percentage of your refund as their fee, as this can incentivize them to take unnecessary risks on your tax return.

Communication is also essential. Look for a tax professional who communicates clearly and promptly. You want someone who will explain complex tax concepts to you in a way that you can understand and who will respond to your questions and concerns in a timely manner. Good communication is especially important if you're working with a tax professional remotely.

Overall, taking the time to select the right tax professional can save you time, money, and stress in the long run. By considering qualifications, reputation, fees, and communication, you can find a tax professional who can help you navigate the complex world of taxes and ensure that you're in compliance with all applicable laws and regulations.

Questions to Ask a Tax Professional

Asking questions is an important step in selecting a tax professional to assist with your taxes. Here are some additional details to consider when asking the questions mentioned above:

Qualifications and experience: When inquiring about a tax professional's qualifications, ask about their education, training, and experience working with individuals or businesses in similar tax situations as yours. Some tax professionals may specialize in certain areas, such as small business taxes, international tax laws, or estate planning. It's important to choose a professional with the right expertise to address your specific tax needs.

Fees: Make sure to ask about the fees upfront and what services are included in those fees. Some tax professionals charge a flat fee for tax preparation services, while others charge an hourly rate. Inquire about any additional fees for services such as tax planning, IRS representation, or audit assistance. Understanding the costs involved will help you make an informed decision about which tax professional to hire.

Communication: Clear communication is essential in any professional relationship, and this is especially true when it comes to taxes. Ask about the tax professional's preferred method of communication, whether it be phone, email, or in-person meetings. Find out how often they typically communicate with clients and their response time to client inquiries. You want to choose a professional who is responsive and communicative throughout the tax preparation process.

Availability during tax season: Tax season can be a busy time for tax professionals, and it's important to find out if they will have the time to dedicate to your tax needs. Ask about their availability during tax season and what their turnaround time is for completing tax returns. Additionally, find out if they have backup support in case they become overwhelmed with their workload.

By asking these questions and carefully considering the answers, you can find a tax professional who is well-qualified, communicates effectively, and is a good fit for your specific tax needs.

Conclusion

Selecting the right tax professional can be crucial for the success of your tax planning and preparation efforts. A tax professional can help you navigate the complex tax laws, identify deductions and credits you may not have been aware of, and ensure that you comply with all tax regulations.

When choosing a tax professional, it's important to consider their qualifications. Some of the most common qualifications include Certified Public Accountant (CPA), Enrolled Agent (EA), and tax attorney. Each of these qualifications has different requirements and areas of expertise, so it's important to choose a professional who has experience in your specific tax situation.

Another important factor to consider is the reputation of the tax professional. You can research their credentials, reviews, and ratings online to get an idea of their reputation in the industry. You can also ask for referrals from friends, family, or colleagues who have used a tax professional before.

Fees are another important consideration when selecting a tax professional. Some tax professionals charge a flat fee, while others charge an hourly rate. It's important to understand how much you will be charged and what services are included in the fee.

Communication is also critical when working with a tax professional. You want someone who is responsive, proactive, and easy to work with. They should be able to explain complex tax issues in a way that is easy to understand and be available to answer your questions throughout the year, not just during tax season.

By taking the time to find a qualified and reputable tax professional, you can ensure that you are getting the best possible advice and guidance when it comes to your taxes. They can provide peace of mind during tax season and help you minimize your tax liabilities while maximizing your tax benefits.

Chapter 7: Understanding Tax Deadlines and Extensions

The tax system has specific deadlines and extensions that taxpayers must be aware of to avoid penalties and interest charges. Filing taxes on time is essential to avoid these penalties and interest charges that can add up quickly. In this chapter, we'll explore the various tax deadlines and extensions you need to be aware of.

The tax year runs from January 1 to December 31, and taxpayers are required to file their tax returns by April 15th of the following year. This means that taxes for the year 2021 must be filed by April 15, 2022. However, if April 15th falls on a weekend or holiday, the deadline is moved to the next business day.

If you cannot file your taxes by the deadline, you can request an extension of time to file. The deadline to request an extension is also April 15th. By filing for an extension, you can extend the filing deadline by six months to October 15th. It's important to note that an extension of time to file does not extend the deadline to pay any taxes owed. Interest and penalties will still accrue on any unpaid tax liability after the original deadline.

Another important deadline to be aware of is the deadline for making contributions to certain retirement accounts, such as traditional and Roth IRAs. The deadline for contributions is usually April 15th of the following year, but it may be extended if the tax filing deadline is extended.

It's important to stay on top of these deadlines and extensions to avoid penalties and interest charges. Missing a deadline can result in costly consequences, so it's always best to file your taxes on time or request an extension if necessary.

Tax Deadlines

The tax deadlines vary depending on the type of taxpayer and the type of tax return being filed.

Tax deadlines are established by the Internal Revenue Service (IRS) and are generally set by law. For example, the deadline for filing federal income tax returns is April 15th of each year, unless that date falls on a weekend or holiday, in which case the deadline is the next business day. The IRS may also grant extensions for filing tax returns, but these extensions do not usually extend the deadline for paying any taxes owed.

The IRS may also establish other deadlines for various tax-related activities, such as filing information returns, making estimated tax payments, or submitting certain tax forms. These deadlines may vary depending on the specific tax form or activity, and it is important to check with the IRS or a tax professional for the specific deadlines that apply to your situation.

It is important to note that missing tax deadlines can result in penalties and interest charges, so it is important to stay organized and aware of all applicable deadlines. For businesses, the tax deadline is typically March 15th for S-corporations and partnerships, and April 15th for C-corporations. Again, if the deadline falls on a weekend or holiday, the deadline is extended to the next business day.

During the pandemic, the IRS and many state tax agencies postponed the traditional April 15th deadline for filing and paying taxes. In 2020, the federal tax deadline was moved to July 15th, giving taxpayers an additional three months to file their tax returns and pay any taxes owed without incurring penalties or interest. This extension applied to individual income tax returns, as well as to many other types of tax returns, including trusts and estates, partnerships, corporations, and nonprofit organizations.

Many states also extended their tax deadlines in response to the pandemic, though the specific dates varied by state. Some states aligned their deadlines with the federal July 15th deadline, while others set their own dates, such as July 1st or July 31st.

In 2021, the IRS announced that the traditional April 15th deadline would be extended to May 17th for individual income tax returns. However, taxpayers who need more time to file their returns can request an extension until October 15th, though any taxes owed must still be paid by May 17th to avoid penalties and interest. State tax agencies may have their own deadlines, so it's important for taxpayers to check with their state tax agency to determine the specific due dates for their returns.

If you are unable to file your tax return by the deadline, you can request an extension.

Individuals can request a six-month extension, which extends the tax deadline from April 15th to October 15th. To request an extension, you must file Form 4868 with the IRS by the original due date of your tax return.

Businesses can also request extensions for their tax returns. For S-corporations and partnerships, the deadline can be extended by six months by filing Form 7004. For C-corporations, the deadline can be extended by five months by filing Form 7004.

It's important to note that while an extension can give you more time to file your tax return, it does not extend the deadline for paying any taxes owed. If you do not pay your taxes by the original deadline, you may still be subject to penalties and interest charges, even if you have been granted an extension to file your return.

Additionally, when requesting an extension, you need to estimate the amount of tax you owe and include that amount when you file Form 4868. If you underestimate the amount of tax owed, you may still face penalties and interest charges.

It's also important to keep in mind that while an extension gives you more time to file your tax return, it doesn't mean you should delay gathering your tax information and documents. Starting early and being prepared can help you avoid a last-minute scramble to file your return or request an extension.

It's also worth noting that certain taxpayers, such as those serving in a combat zone, may be eligible for an extension beyond the six-month automatic extension. They can check the IRS website for more information and forms specific to their situation.

The interest charges begin accruing from the original tax deadline, regardless of any extensions granted. This means that even if you file for an extension, you will still be subject to interest charges if you do not pay any taxes owed by the original deadline.

If you fail to file your tax return and owe taxes, the penalty for failing to file is typically more severe than the penalty for failing to pay. This is because the IRS wants taxpayers to at least file their return, even if they are unable to pay the full amount owed.

It's important to note that there are some circumstances in which the IRS may waive penalties for late filing or late payment. For example, if you have a valid reason for not being able to file or pay on time, such as a natural disaster or serious illness, you may be able to request penalty relief. However, interest charges will still apply.

To avoid penalties and interest charges, it's important to file your tax return on time and pay any taxes owed by the deadline. If you are unable to pay the full amount owed, you can still file your return and set up a payment plan with the IRS to pay off the balance over time. This can help you avoid more severe penalties and interest charges.

Conclusion

Staying organized and aware of tax deadlines and extensions is crucial to avoid penalties and interest charges from the IRS. Missing the tax deadline or failing to pay any taxes owed can result in hefty penalties and interest charges, which can quickly add up and significantly increase the amount owed to the IRS.

To avoid these penalties and interest charges, it's essential to mark the tax deadline on your calendar and ensure that you file your tax return on time. If you are unable to file by the deadline, consider requesting an extension by filing Form 4868. However, keep in mind that an extension only extends the deadline for filing your tax return, not for paying any taxes owed. Thus, it's crucial to pay any taxes owed by the tax deadline to avoid penalties and interest charges.

To help ensure that you don't miss any tax deadlines, it's also helpful to stay organized and keep track of your tax-related documents and deadlines throughout the year. This can include setting reminders on your calendar or using tax software that can help you keep track of deadlines and file your tax return electronically.

Overall, by staying organized, aware of tax deadlines, and paying any taxes owed on time, you can ensure that you are meeting your tax obligations and avoiding unnecessary fees and penalties.

Special Circumstances for Service Members

Service members and their families have unique tax situations that require special attention. Whether they are active duty, reserve, or retired, service members face different tax rules and regulations than civilians. In this essay, we will explore some of the ways in which service members' taxes differ from those of civilians.

One of the biggest differences in tax rules for service members is their ability to exclude certain types of pay from their taxable income. For example, combat pay, also known as hazardous duty pay, is tax-free. Service members can exclude this pay from their taxable income, which can result in a lower tax bill. Additionally, any allowances that service members receive for housing and meals are also tax-free, ~~as long as~~ if they are on active duty and stationed outside the United States.

Another way in which service members' taxes differ from civilians is their ability to claim certain tax credits. For example, service members who adopt a child while on active duty can claim the adoption tax credit, which can help offset the costs associated with adopting a child. Additionally, service members who are called to active duty in a combat zone can claim the Earned Income Tax Credit (EITC), which can provide a substantial tax refund.

Service members who move frequently may also be eligible for certain tax deductions. For example, if a service member is required to move to a new duty station, they may be able to deduct the expenses associated with moving, such as the cost of packing and shipping household goods. Additionally, service members who are required to maintain a home in one location while serving in another location may be able to deduct the expenses associated with maintaining that home, such as mortgage interest and property taxes.

Service members also have special rules for filing their taxes. For example, service members who are deployed outside the United States on the regular tax filing deadline are automatically granted a two-month extension to file their taxes. Additionally, service members who are unable to file their taxes on time due to military service can request an additional extension. This can be helpful for service members who are deployed or who are otherwise unable to file their taxes on time.

In conclusion, service members have different tax rules and regulations than civilians. They may be able to exclude certain types of pay from their taxable income, claim certain tax credits, and deduct certain expenses related to military service. Additionally, service members have special rules for filing their taxes, including extensions for those who are deployed or otherwise unable to file on time. By understanding these unique tax rules and regulations, service members can take advantage of the tax benefits available to them and ensure that they are meeting their tax obligations.

The Affordable Care Act (ACA), also known as Obamacare, is a healthcare reform law that was signed into law in 2010. The ACA was designed to increase access to healthcare and reduce the overall cost of healthcare in the United States. The law has had a significant impact on the healthcare industry and on the taxes that individuals and businesses must pay.

One of the key provisions of the ACA is the individual mandate, which requires individuals to have health insurance or pay a penalty. The penalty for not having insurance is calculated based on the individual's income and can be significant. The individual mandate was implemented to encourage more people to obtain health insurance and reduce the number of uninsured individuals in the country.

The ACA also created a number ofseveral tax credits and subsidies to help individuals and families afford health insurance. These tax credits are available to individuals who purchase insurance through the health insurance marketplace and meet certain income requirements. The amount of the tax credit is based on the individual's income and the cost of the insurance plan.

For businesses, the ACA introduced the employer mandate, which requires businesses with 50 or more full-time employees to provide health insurance to their employees or pay a penalty. The employer mandate was implemented to ensure that more individuals have access to health insurance through their employer.

The ACA also made changes to the way that healthcare providers are reimbursed for their services. The law introduced the Medicare Access and CHIP Reauthorization Act (MACRA), which created a new payment system for healthcare providers. The new payment system is designed to reward providers for providing high-quality care and achieving positive health outcomes for their patients.

In addition to these provisions, the ACA also includes a number of other changes to the healthcare system. These include new requirements for insurance companies, changes to Medicaid and Medicare, and increased funding for preventative care services.

Overall, the ACA has had a significant impact on the healthcare industry and on the taxes that individuals and businesses must pay. While the law has been controversial, it has helped to increase access to healthcare and reduce the overall cost of healthcare in the United States. As with any major healthcare reform, there have been challenges in implementing the law, but it has made important strides in improving healthcare for millions of Americans.

Helpful Vocabulary

1. Taxpayer - a person or organization that pays taxes to the government

2. Income - money earned or received, usually through work or investments

3. Taxable income - the portion of income that is subject to taxation

4. Tax deduction - a reduction in taxable income that lowers the amount of taxes owed

5. Tax credit - a dollar-for-dollar reduction in the amount of taxes owed

6. Tax bracket - a range of income levels that are taxed at a specific rate

7. Tax liability - the total amount of taxes owed to the government

8. Tax refund - a reimbursement from the government for overpaid taxes

9. W-2 form - a document provided by employers that shows an employee's wages and taxes withheld for the year

10. 1099 form - a document provided by employers or other payers that shows non-wage income, such as freelance earnings or investment income

11. Standard deduction - a fixed amount of tax deduction that can be claimed without itemizing deductions

12. Itemized deductions - expenses that can be deducted from taxable income, such as charitable donations or mortgage interest

13. Dependent - a person who relies on another person for financial support, such as a child or elderly parent

14. Taxable event - a transaction or activity that results in a tax liability, such as selling a stock or receiving rental income

15. Capital gains - the profit earned from selling an asset, such as stocks or real estate

16. Tax-exempt - income or transactions that are not subject to taxation

17. Tax-deferred - income or transactions that are not subject to taxation until a later date, such as retirement savings

18. Audit - an examination of tax returns by the government to ensure accuracy and compliance with tax laws

19. Penalty - a fee charged for failing to comply with tax laws or filing deadlines

20. Interest - a charge applied to unpaid taxes or penalties, typically calculated as a percentage of the amount owed

21. Tax credit: A dollar-for-dollar reduction in the amount of taxes owed, based on specific criteria such as income level or expenses incurred.

22. Tax deduction: An expense that can be subtracted from taxable income to reduce the amount of taxes owed.

23. Taxable income: The amount of income subject to taxation after subtracting any deductions and exemptions.

24. Tax liability: The amount of taxes owed to the government based on income, deductions, and credits.

25. Depreciation: A tax deduction that allows businesses to write off the cost of a long-term asset over time.

26. Capital gains: Profits made from the sale of assets, such as stocks or real estate, that are subject to taxation.

27. Withholding: The amount of taxes that an employer deducts from an employee's paycheck and remits to the government on their behalf.

28. Standard deduction: A set amount that can be subtracted from taxable income without having to itemize deductions.

29. Itemized deduction: A list of specific expenses that can be subtracted from taxable income to reduce the amount of taxes owed.

30. Tax bracket: A range of income levels that determines the rate at which taxes are assessed.

30.

Formatted: Normal, Indent: Left: 0.25", No bullets or numbering

Formatted: Normal, Indent: Left: 0.25", Line spacing: Double

Important Forms you May Need

1. Form 1040: U.S. Individual Income Tax Return

2. Form 1040-SR: U.S. Tax Return for Seniors

3. Form 1040-ES: Estimated Tax for Individuals

4. Form W-2: Wage and Tax Statement

5. Form W-4: Employee's Withholding Allowance Certificate

6. Form 1099-MISC: Miscellaneous Income

7. Form 1099-INT: Interest Income

8. Form 1099-DIV: Dividends and Distributions

9. Form 1099-R: Distributions from Pensions, Annuities, Retirement or Profit-Sharing Plans, IRAs, Insurance Contracts, etc.

Believe it or not, record keeping doesn't have to be crazy. Really all the IRS wants to see is some
organization so that you can tie your expenses to receipts. A form as simple as the one below
can serve to work wonders to get you ready for tax time, or keep you ready for an audit. Think
of an audit as no more than showing your work – and you'll nail it.

Important Forms you May Need

1. Form 1040: U.S. Individual Income Tax Return

2. Form 1040-SR: U.S. Tax Return for Seniors

3. Form 1040-ES: Estimated Tax for Individuals

4. Form W-2: Wage and Tax Statement

5. Form W-4: Employee's Withholding Allowance Certificate

6. Form 1099-MISC: Miscellaneous Income

7. Form 1099-INT: Interest Income

8. Form 1099-DIV: Dividends and Distributions

9. Form 1099-R: Distributions from Pensions, Annuities, Retirement or Profit-Sharing Plans,
IRAs, Insurance Contracts, etc.

10. Form 1098: Mortgage Interest Statement

11. Form 4562: Depreciation and Amortization

12. Form 8863: Education Credits (American Opportunity and Lifetime Learning Credits)

13. Form 8962: Premium Tax Credit (PTC)

14. Form 8965: Health Coverage Exemptions

15. Form 3520: Annual Return to Report Transactions With Foreign Trusts and Receipt of
Certain Foreign Gifts

Date	Expense	Amount	Business Purpose	Notes